I CAN BE A WRITER

I Can Be a Poet

Meeg Pincus

Published in the United States of America by:

CHERRY LAKE PRESS
2395 South Huron Parkway, Suite 200, Ann Arbor, Michigan 48104
www.cherrylakepress.com

Reading Adviser: Beth Walker Gambro, MS, Ed., Reading Consultant, Yorkville, IL

Photo Credits: © nito/Shutterstock, 5; Wikimedia Commons by CC0 1.0 Universal, 6; © Hoika Mikhail/Shutterstock, 7; Various illustrations via Shutterstock, 8; © ZUMA Press, Inc./Alamy Stock Photo, 9; © Bob Daemmrich/Alamy Stock Photo, 11; © EWY Media/Shutterstock, 12; Wikimedia Commons by CC0 1.0 Universal, 13; © metamorworks/Shutterstock, 15; © PeopleImages.com - Yuri A/Shutterstock, 16; © Evgeny Atamanenko/Shutterstock, 18; © Maxim Elramsisy/Shutterstock, 20; © Westlight/Shutterstock, 21; © Crazy nook/Shutterstock, 22

Copyright © 2026 by Cherry Lake Publishing Group

All rights reserved. No part of this book may be reproduced or utilized in any form or by any means without written permission from the publisher.

Cherry Lake Press is an imprint of Cherry Lake Publishing Group.

Library of Congress Cataloging-in-Publication Data has been filed and is available at catalog.loc.gov

Cherry Lake Publishing Group would like to acknowledge the work of the Partnership for 21st Century Learning, a Network of Battelle for Kids. Please visit Battelle for Kids online for more information.

Printed in the United States of America

Note from publisher: Websites change regularly, and their future contents are outside of our control. Supervise children when conducting any recommended online searches for extended learning opportunities.

CONTENTS

What Do Poets Do?	4
Why Would I Want to Write Poetry?	10
How Can I Learn to Write Poetry?	17
Activity	22
Find Out More	23
About the Author	23
Glossary	24
Index	24

WHAT DO POETS DO?

Did you love nursery rhymes as a toddler? Have you ever giggled at a funny **limerick**? Have you read a great **novel in verse**?

Then you've seen what poets do!

Poets write poems. These are a type of artistic writing that aims to stir a reader's imagination and emotions. A poet carefully chooses and arranges words for their meaning, sound, and **rhythm**.

Poetry is the oldest known form of writing. Archaeologists have found poems etched into clay tablets from ancient times.

This ancient Sumerian tablet is over 4,000 years old. It is a love poem to King Shu-Sin.

Make a Guess!

Why do you think poetry is the oldest form of writing? If you guessed that it was because it could be sung and performed, you are right!

Today, poets still exist. Some write poetry as a job. Many write poetry as a hobby, just for themselves, or to share with close friends and family. Either way, poets write poetry to express themselves.

Most professional poets work freelance. That means they have their own businesses, usually at home. They send their poems to various places to try to get them published.

Poems may be published in books or magazines, or on art like greeting cards or posters. Poets may give readings for public events. They may also teach poetry or English classes. Some write other things as well.

Some poets compete in poetry slams in front of judges.

WHY WOULD I WANT TO WRITE POETRY?

Do you have strong emotions you want to express? Do you love to be extra creative with words? Can you hear the sounds and rhythms of language?

Then you may want to write poetry!

Ask Questions!

Write a letter to a poet. Ask what they like about writing poetry or how they knew they wanted to write poetry. Ask any questions you have for them!

William Shakespeare was a playwright and poet. He wrote famous sonnets.

Poets get to play with words. There are so many types of poetry to play with, from **haiku** to **sonnets**.

Each type of poem has its own format. Some types have rules, like a specific number of lines that must rhyme. Others have no real rules at all, like **free verse**. As a poet, you get to be creative in trying these different ways of writing.

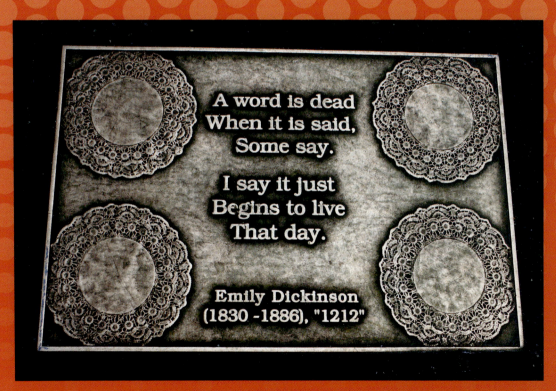

A poet may be invited to read their writing aloud. This is the best way to share the sounds and rhythms of most poems. Poets often choose words for what they sound like and how they sound together.

All the five senses are a big part of writing poetry. Do you like to make readers feel, smell, see, taste, and hear with your words? Then you might just be a poet!

Look!

Some poems also need to be seen, like concrete poems and acrostic poems. Find some and see how visual poetry can be!

Poets can capture moments in time and share them with the world.

HOW CAN I LEARN TO WRITE POETRY?

How many poems have you read? The best poets read lots of poetry!

Go to the library and check out poetry books. Ask for poetry books or magazines as gifts. Read different kinds of poetry to get a feel for what you like. The more poetry you read, the better poet and writer you will become.

Where do you feel inspired?

It takes time to figure out what kind of poetry you enjoy writing.

You may find you're a silly poet who loves writing limericks. You may be a nature-loving poet who writes haiku. Or maybe you'll be a storytelling poet who writes novels in verse.

The only way to know is to write poems. Write a poem when you have strong feelings or a moment of wonder. Write many poems, and write them often!

Create!

Make your own poetry journal, where you can write poems. You can also add images, which you can create or cut out from magazines.

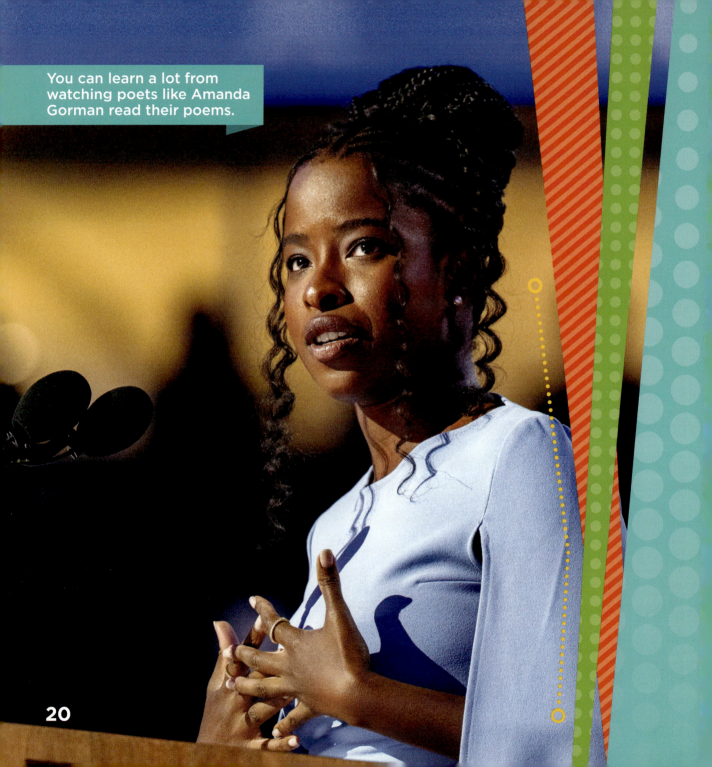

You can learn a lot from watching poets like Amanda Gorman read their poems.

You can take classes in poetry. You can enter poetry writing contests or submit poems to magazines. You can write poems as gifts for family and friends.

Can you be a poet? If you want to express yourself through wordplay and turn emotions into creative writing... yes, you can!

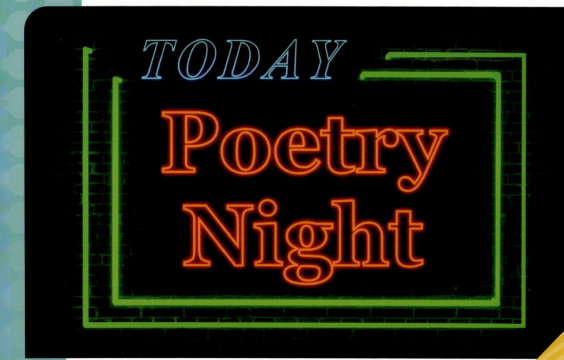

ACTIVITY

Not sure whether you can write a poem? Try this!

Write a simple poem that begins with one of these two sentences:

- I cannot write a poem today.

- I have to write a poem, but how?

Your poem can rhyme, like this:

I cannot write a poem today,
so I'll just push that thought away.
I'd rather go outside and play,
than try to write a poem today.

Or it can be in free verse, not rhyming, like this:

I have to write a poem, but how?
Will its words pop into my head?
Dance upon my heart?
Tickle my ear with humor?
Burst out of my mouth full of feeling?
I have to write a poem,
so I guess I'll just wait
and see what happens.

Your poem can be as short as four lines or as long as you like. Remember to have fun—poetry is just playing with words!

FIND OUT MORE

Books

Alexander, Kwame, and Deanna Nikaido. *How to Write a Poem.* New York, NY: HarperCollins, 2023.

Martin, Jerome. *Write Your Own Poems.* London, UK: Usborne, 2024.

Websites

With an adult, explore more online with these suggested searches.

"A Poem by Youth Poet Laureate Elizabeth Acevedo," *YouTube*

"A Poetry Lesson with Newbery Medal Winner Kwame Alexander," *YouTube*

"Inaugural Poet Amanda Gorman Reads Her Poem/Picture Book," *YouTube*

"On Poetry with Youth Poet Laureate Joy Harjo," *YouTube*

"Shel Silverstein Performs His Poems," *Shel Silverstein* site

ABOUT THE AUTHOR

Meeg Pincus loves to write. She is the author of more than 30 books for children. She has been a writer and editor for books, newspapers, magazines, and more. She also loves to sing, make art, and hang out with her family, friends, and adorable dog.

GLOSSARY

acrostic poems (uh-KRAW-stik POH-uhms) poems where the first letter of each line spells out a word

concrete poems (KAHN-kreet POH-uhms) poems that arrange words in a shape to create an image

free verse (FREE VUHRS) open form of poetry with no set rules

haiku (HIE-koo) Japanese style of poem with three lines and a specific number of syllables

limerick (LIH-muh-rik) funny, light-hearted poem with five lines and specific rhyme rules

novel in verse (NAH-vuhl IN VUHRS) long, fictional story written in poetry

rhythm (RIH-thuhm) regular pattern of repeating sounds and beats

sonnets (SAH-nuhts) poems with 14 lines and specific rhyme rules

INDEX

activities, 22
ancient poetry, 6, 7

Dickinson, Emily, 13

education, 17, 20–21

forms and formats, 6, 9, 12–13, 14, 22
free verse, 13, 22

Gorman, Amanda, 20

journaling, 19

learning, 17–21

poetry, 4–7, 10, 12–13, 14, 17, 19–21, 22
poets, 4
  activities, 22
  emulation, 11, 17, 20
  motivation, 4, 7, 10–15, 19, 21
  types, 8, 9, 19

public readings, 9, 11, 14, 20
publishing, 8–9, 21

reading habits, 17
readings, 9, 11, 14, 20
rhyme, 13, 22

senses, 14
Shakespeare, William, 12

visual poetry, 14

writing poetry, 4, 7, 10–14, 17–21, 22

24